INDE

PAGE	

INDEX

PAGE	

INDEX

PAGE	

INDEX

PAGE	

20879628R00070

Printed in Great Britain
by Amazon